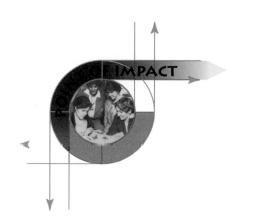

The Nineteenth Amendment

Women Get the Vote

KAREN PRICE HOSSELL

Heinemann Library
Chicago, Illinois

© 2003 Reed Educational & Professional Publishing
Published by Heinemann Library,
an imprint of Reed Educational & Professional Publishing,
Chicago, Illinois

Customer Service 888-454-2279

Visit our website at www.heinemannlibrary.com

Designed by Roslyn Broder
Printed in the United States by Lake Book Manufacturing, Inc.

07 06 05 04 03
10 9 8 7 6 5 4 3 2 1

Library of Congress Cataloging-in-Publication Data
Price Hossell, Karen, 1957-
   The nineteenth amendment : women get the vote / by Karen Price
Hossell.
       v. cm. -- (Point of impact)
Includes bibliographical references (p.) and index.
Contents: Women get the vote -- The rights of women in early America --
The first women's rights conference -- The fight for human rights --
Fighters for the cause -- The fourteenth and fifteenth amendments -- The
movement divides -- The new suffragists -- Women in World War I --
Ratification -- The equal rights amendment -- Women make a difference --
Women in government -- Important dates -- Glossary.
  ISBN 1-58810-908-9 (HC), 1-40340-535-2 (Pbk)
  1. Women--Suffrage--United States--History--Juvenile literature. [1.
Women--Suffrage. 2. Women's rights--History.] I. Title. II. Series.
  JK1898 .P75 2002
  324.6'23'0973--dc21
                              2001008697

Acknowledgments
The author and publishers are grateful to the following for permission to reproduce copyright material:
pp. 4, 8, 9, 12, 15, 17, 18, 21 The Library of Congress, Print and Photographs Division; pp. 5, 14 AP/Wide World Photos; pp. 6, 7 Christie's Images/Corbis; pp. 10, 13, 16, 19 , 25, 26, 28 Bettmann/Corbis; pp. 11, 27 Hulton-Deutsch/Corbis; pp. 20, 23, 24 Corbis; p. 29 AFP/Corbis.

Cover photograph by (T-B): The Library of Congress, Print and Photographs Division; Corbis.

Every effort has been made to contact copyright holders of any material reproduced in this book. Any omissions will be rectified in subsequent printings if notice is given to the publisher.

The author would like to thank her parents, her husband, David, and her editor, Angela McHaney Brown.

Some words are shown in bold, **like this.** You can find out what they mean by looking in the glossary.

Contents

Women Get the Vote

On August 26, 1920, in Washington, D.C., bells rang and whistles blew. Secretary of State Bainbridge Colby had just issued a **proclamation** declaring that the Nineteenth **Amendment** had been **ratified** and was now part of the United States Constitution. Women hugged and cried. They and women before them had worked so long and hard for **suffrage**—the right to vote—and their goal had finally been achieved.

It had been a difficult, 72-year-long battle. Many women had dedicated their lives to it. They had made speeches, collected signatures on **petitions,** spoken to members of Congress, and marched in the streets. They had protested, been arrested, and gone on hunger strikes. But the battle was finally over.

In 1912, women marched together in parades in New York seeking the right to vote.

The amendment to give women the right to vote was first introduced to Congress in 1878. It was reintroduced in every session of Congress for 40 years. Congress rejected it until 1919, when it was approved as the Nineteenth Amendment to the Constitution. The amendment states: "The right of citizens of the United States to vote shall not be denied or abridged by the United States or by any State on account of sex. Congress shall have power to enforce this article by appropriate legislation."

Before 1920, other countries had given women the vote. In New Zealand, for example, women could vote starting in 1893. In Australia, they could vote in national elections in 1903, and in Finland, women could vote as of 1906. In four U.S. states, women could vote in all elections. In some states, they could vote in some elections, but not all of them. There was no federal amendment that granted women the right to vote. Some of them tried and were turned away from the polls, or arrested and fined.

People against suffrage

Many people fought against giving women the vote. These people, called **antisuffragists,** believed that women should stay at home to take care of their children, clean house, and cook meals. They believed that only men should govern the nation.

Businesses also fought against suffrage for women. The liquor industry, for example, feared that women would approve **prohibition** laws. Those laws would make it illegal to make or sell alcoholic beverages. Other industries were also against giving women the vote. Owners of factories knew that if women could vote they would make laws to improve working conditions, and the new laws would cost the factories money.

WHAT IS AN AMENDMENT?

An amendment to the United States Constitution is a change in a law. Congress can propose an amendment after two-thirds of both houses of Congress the House of Representatives and the Senate—approve it. Another way Congress can propose an amendment is if two-thirds of the states have formally requested it. When states are presented with an amendment, they usually have seven years to approve or reject it. Three-fourths of the states must approve an amendment for it to pass. There have been 27 amendments to the Constitution.

In this 1918 suffrage parade in New York, people carried signs saying, "Let New York Be Next."

The Rights of Women in Early America

Women in early America had few rights. If a married woman worked outside the home, for example, her husband owned any money she earned. Women who wanted to go to a college or university had few choices. The first university to admit women, Oberlin College in Ohio, did not open its classes to women until 1834.

When a married woman's husband died, she did not get his property. Instead, it went to her oldest son. If a son and mother were not on good terms, he could ask his mother to leave the house. When a married woman's father died, anything she inherited automatically went to her husband. Divorce was rare in early America. Women who did divorce, though, could not get **custody** of their children—the father was always awarded custody.

Women could not vote and had no say in the laws that were made, but they were forced to obey them. They were regarded as more religious than men and able to lead good, pure lives. The world of politics was considered unclean—a place for strong men, not women.

Many women in the 1800s spent most of their time doing household chores such as sewing. Some women earned a small income from their sewing.

Owning property

Some **reforms** were made in 1839, when Mississippi became the first state to pass a Married Women's Property Act. The act allowed women to inherit slaves. In 1848, New York passed the act. The New York version allowed women to keep property that was inherited or received as a gift. Still, a woman could not sell the property without her husband's signature. The Tennessee **legislature** rejected the act in 1849, stating that because women had no souls, they had no right to own property.

Women were expected to do most of the cooking and cleaning in households in the 1800s.

RESISTING WOMEN'S SUFFRAGE

The words below are from a letter written by an **antisuffragist** named Kelly Miller and published in the women's **suffrage** magazine *The Crisis*. His words show how many men and women felt about the struggle for women to get the vote:

Woman is physically weaker than man and is incapable of competing with him in the stern and strenuous activities of public and practical life…She lacks the sharp sense of public justice and the common good, if they seem to run counter to her personal feeling and interest. She is far superior to man in purely personal and private virtue, but is his inferior in public qualities and character. Suffrage is not a natural right, like life and liberty.

The First Woman's Rights Convention

Elizabeth Cady was born in 1815 in Johnstown, New York. Her father was a successful attorney. When Elizabeth was a young girl, she would sit in a corner of his office while he worked and listen to the women who came to him for help. Some of them were widows who had lost their homes when their husbands died. Some had husbands who worked but used all the money they made to buy liquor, leaving none to buy food and clothes for their children.

Elizabeth Cady Stanton is shown here with her daughter, Harriot.

Elizabeth quietly watched as her father turned the women away, telling them that he was sorry, but there was nothing he could do to help them. When Elizabeth questioned her father, he told her that when she got older she should go to Albany, the capital of New York, and talk to the **legislators** there about changing the laws.

When Elizabeth was a young woman, she married Henry Brewster Stanton, an **abolitionist.** While most women promised to obey their husbands when they got married, Elizabeth insisted that the word "obey" be taken out of her marriage vows. She also chose to keep her maiden name—the name she had before she was married—and was always known as Elizabeth Cady Stanton.

Forbidden to participate

The Stantons traveled to London, England, to attend the first World Anti-Slavery Convention. There, Elizabeth met Lucretia Mott, another abolitionist. At the convention, all of the women were told that they could not participate as the men could. They were forced to sit behind a curtain so they could not be seen. This led Stanton and Mott to have a long talk about women's rights. Before they left London, they promised that when they got back to the United States they would form a society for women's rights.

The convention

They finally formed the society in 1848, when they organized a Woman's Rights Convention in Seneca Falls, New York, where Elizabeth lived. The more than 300 women at the convention voted to approve a Declaration of Sentiments, a list of statements telling what they hoped to do. The declaration was based on the Declaration of Independence, but specifically addressed women's rights. It included the fact that women were not allowed to vote, yet they were forced to obey laws that they had no voice in making.

Besides helping Stanton to organize the women's rights movement, Lucretia Mott also established two antislavery groups. These were the American Anti-Slavery Society and the Philadelphia Female Anti-Slavery Society.

The women came up with twelve items called **resolutions.** One, the ninth resolution, caused some differences of opinion. It stated that women had a duty to fight for the right to vote. Some of the women at the convention thought this went too far and would make the entire society look ridiculous for even mentioning it. Henry Stanton had left town during the convention because of the resolution, claiming that he did not want to be associated with it. Elizabeth, though, kept insisting that the ninth resolution be included. So did Frederick Douglass, a well-known African-American abolitionist and speaker who attended the conference. Because of their persistence, the resolution was approved, although many still voted against it.

The Fight for Human Rights

The antislavery movement, or **abolitionist** movement, was the first human rights effort in the United States. It began when religious groups such as the Baptists, **Quakers,** and Presbyterians came together to argue that in God's eyes all humans were equal. The movement began in the 1820s when religious groups organized antislavery societies. Society members printed and distributed literature on why slavery was immoral, and they held public meetings to speak out against it.

In the 1840s, about the time of the first Woman's Rights Convention, the antislavery movement also took up the issue of women's rights. Quakers, in particular, treated women and men as equals and spoke out against the injustices women faced. Many early **suffragists** were also abolitionists.

LADIES' DEPARTMENT.

'Am I not a Woman and a Sister?'

White Lady, happy, proud and free,
Lend awhile thine ear to me ;
Let the Negro Mother's wail
Turn thy pale cheek still more pale.
Can the Negro Mother joy
Over this her captive boy,
Which in bondage and in tears,
For a life of wo she rears?
Though she bears a Mother's name,
A Mother's rights she may not claim ;
For the white man's will can part,
Her darling from her bursting heart.

From the Genius of Universal Emancipation
LETTERS ON SLAVERY.—No. III.

This 1849 poem and illustration called for all women to join the cause against slavery.

Women's Christian Temperance Union

Another movement that lent its support to women's **suffrage** was the Women's Christian **Temperance** Union (WCTU). This organization was formed in 1874 to address the problem of alcohol abuse in the United States. Soon many countries had branches of the union.

In the 1800s, alcohol was a popular drink any time of the day. Few women drank until they were drunk, but so many men did after the **Civil War** that it became a national problem. Men were neglecting their families to go off drinking for hours, days, or even weeks. Members of the WCTU would go into **saloons** and kneel down and pray, asking God to help those inside to stop drinking. They also begged saloon owners to stop selling liquor. The women were almost always laughed at, ignored, or called names.

In 1880, a woman named Frances Willard became president of the WCTU. She and the other members soon became frustrated by their lack of power and began to realize that the only way they would achieve their goal of **prohibition**—making the sale of alcoholic beverages illegal—was if they could vote. Because the members were religious, they soon began persuading one another that it was their Christian duty to support suffrage.

The support of the WCTU brought many new members into the fight for women's suffrage. Most of the women in the WCTU would not have joined the effort otherwise, because suffrage leaders were considered unfeminine and radical. With their support, the suffrage movement was energized.

Francis Willard and other members of the WCTU called their suffrage program Home Protection, because they believed voting would help them protect their homes from drunkenness. Their motto became "Woman will bless and brighten every place she enters, and she will enter every place."

Fighters for the Cause

American women spoke out for their rights from the country's earliest days. Elizabeth Cady Stanton and Lucretia Mott, most of all, are usually thought of as the women who started the women's rights and **suffrage** movements when they arranged the first Women's Rights Convention in 1848.

Susan B. Anthony

Another **suffragist,** Susan B. Anthony, worked closely with Stanton from the time they met in 1851 until Stanton's death in 1902. Stanton was married and had seven children, whereas Anthony remained unmarried. She spent much of her time traveling and making speeches calling for women's suffrage.

Lucy Stone

Lucy Stone formed the American Woman Suffrage Association (AWSA) in 1869 and was the editor of *Woman's Journal,* which was the official newspaper of the group. She married Henry Blackwell in 1855 and kept her maiden name, a decision that was shocking to many people at the time. Their daughter, Alice Stone Blackwell, continued her parents' fight for human rights and was also an editor of *Woman's Journal.*

Sojourner Truth

In 1843, a former slave named Isabella renamed herself Sojourner Truth. The word *sojourner* means "traveler." Isabella changed her name because she felt God had given her a mission to travel the country and show people the truth about themselves. Sojourner Truth became a speaker for the **abolitionist** movement and later spoke at women's suffrage meetings as well.

Sojourner Truth was a suffragist as well as an abolitionist.

Frederick Douglass

Frederick Douglass was born in 1818 to a slave woman living near Baltimore, Maryland. When his mother's master died, Douglass ran away to freedom. Douglass worked at the docks in New Bedford, Massachusetts, but his excellent speaking skills brought him to the attention of abolitionists. They asked him to speak at their meetings, and soon he began lecturing for the Massachusetts Anti-Slavery Society.

Frederick Douglass was often criticized for supporting women's suffrage rather than focusing on the abolition of slavery. But he believed all people were entitled to certain rights, including the right to vote. Douglass made substantial contributions to the early cause of women's suffrage.

Douglass supported the cause of women's suffrage, but broke with the women's movement in 1869 when Congress was working on the Fourteenth Amendment to the Constitution. The amendment declared anyone born in the United States to be a citizen of the country, entitled to all the rights of a citizen.

Although the amendment did not state it specifically, this included the right to vote. But Congress later added the word *male* to the amendment so that it ensured the rights of only male citizens. Douglass would not support Stanton and Anthony's fight to remove *male* from the Fourteenth Amendment. He was happy that it gave voting rights to African-American males and was afraid that would be taken away if he joined the women's fight, so the three parted ways.

The Fourteenth and Fifteenth Amendments

During the **Civil War,** which lasted from 1861 to 1865, women's **suffrage** was put on hold. As their husbands went off to war, however, women began to prove that they could take on the responsibilities that men once had. They took over businesses and farms, headed large families, and worked at jobs that had once been thought of as only for men.

The Fourteenth Amendment

Slavery was outlawed in the United States by the Thirteenth **Amendment** to the U.S. Constitution, but the amendment did not address the rights of former slaves. After the war ended in 1865, Congress corrected this by passing the Fourteenth Amendment. Section 1 of that amendment states: "All persons born or naturalized in the United States and subject to the jurisdiction thereof, are citizens of the United States and of the State wherein they reside." Section 1 goes on to say that no state should make any law that takes away the privileges of citizens.

Suffragists, though, were not happy when Section 2 of the amendment gave the right to vote to "male inhabitants" only. They argued that they were citizens as stated in Section 1, but because they were women, they were not allowed to practice one of their rights—the right to vote. Suffragists fought to have the wording of the amendment changed.

At the Eleventh Annual National Women's Rights Convention in 1866, Susan B. Anthony proposed that the antislavery movement and the women's movement

The Nineteenth Amendment is sometimes called the Susan B. Anthony Amendment because of the large role she played in getting it passed. A former schoolteacher, Anthony traveled the country giving lectures. She fought for the rights of women until her death in 1906 at the age of 86.

be merged, since they were both fighting for suffrage. The goal of the new organization, called the American Equal Rights Association, was **universal suffrage.** At the convention, Elizabeth Cady Stanton and Susan B. Anthony circulated a **petition** to present to Congress, insisting that the word *male* be removed from the Fourteenth Amendment. About 10,000 people signed the petition. The two women spoke at state **legislatures** that were reviewing the amendment before **ratifying** it. But their efforts to have the word removed were unsuccessful. The Fourteenth Amendment was ratified on July 9, 1868, with the text unchanged.

The Fifteenth Amendment

In 1869 Congress passed the Fifteenth Amendment, and in 1870 it was ratified. The amendment states: "The right of citizens of the United States to vote shall not be denied or abridged by the United States or by any State on account of race, color, or previous condition of servitude." The amendment guaranteed suffrage for African Americans, but not for women.

Women vote

Many suffragists felt that while the Fourteenth and Fifteenth Amendments did not allow women to vote, they should be able to vote because they were citizens. In the presidential election of 1872, Susan B. Anthony and others decided to test the wording of these amendments. She went to the polls in Rochester, New York, and voted. She was arrested two weeks later, found guilty, and fined $100, which she refused to pay. That amount of money would have been like paying $1,450 today.

Anthony was not the first woman to try to vote. Sojourner Truth attempted to vote in the 1872 election in Battle Creek, Michigan. In 1871, in New York City, twelve women tried to vote. One of them succeeded. Also in the year 1871, about 200 African-American women dressed as men were allowed to vote in Johnson County, North Carolina.

Beginning in 1868, many women attempted to vote or to register to vote. In November 1868, Lucy Stone tried to vote in Roseville, New Jersey, but was unsuccessful.

The Movement Divides

The National Woman Suffrage Association

In May 1869, the American Equal Rights Association met in New York City. Much of the discussion was about the recent passage of the Fifteenth **Amendment.** The association became divided over whether to speak out against the amendment. Elizabeth Cady Stanton, the association's president, opposed it, as did Susan B. Anthony. Some people in the crowd booed the two women, accusing them of being racist. Someone suggested that a **resolution** be drawn up to force them to leave the association.

The resolution did not pass, but when the meeting was over, Stanton and Anthony decided to form a separate group, to be based in New York. They called the new organization the National Woman **Suffrage** Association (NWSA). A few months earlier, Stanton had written a sixteenth amendment stating that women were entitled to vote. The passage of the

This illustration shows a NWSA meeting held during an 1880 political convention in Chicago, Illinois.

16

amendment became the goal of the NWSA. The new association quickly signed up about 100 members.

The American Woman Suffrage Association

Some women, though, did not agree with the goals of the NWSA. Stanton had begun speaking out for new laws that would make it easier for women to divorce their husbands, and some women thought she went too far. While they wanted the right to vote, they did not agree with all of her views. Stanton and the NWSA also got involved with other issues, including equal pay.

A group of women wanted to focus solely on getting the vote. Lucy Stone and her husband, Henry Blackwell, formed a suffrage association with Julia Ward Howe in 1869. Their organization, the American Woman Suffrage Association (AWSA), focused on gaining suffrage through state **legislatures** rather than federal legislatures. The AWSA was based in Boston, Massachusetts.

A breakthrough

Meanwhile, one United States territory—Wyoming—had given women the right to vote. When Wyoming became a state in 1890, women's suffrage was kept. That meant women in Wyoming could vote before they could in any other present-day state.

Julia Ward Howe was an **abolitionist** and may be best known today for writing the song "The Battle Hymn of the Republic."

The New Suffragists

In 1890, the American Woman **Suffrage** Association and the National Woman Suffrage Association united to become the National American Woman Suffrage Association (NAWSA). Elizabeth Cady Stanton was president of the association until 1892, when Susan B. Anthony took over. Carrie Chapman Catt was president from 1900 to 1904, and again from 1915 to 1920. Catt decided that the NAWSA would focus on getting the federal **amendment** for women's suffrage passed.

The National Woman's Party

Other members of the association had become frustrated by the lack of progress toward getting women the vote. One of them, Alice Paul, formed a new group in 1916, called the National Woman's Party. On President Woodrow Wilson's inauguration day in 1913, Paul led 8,000 women through the streets in a suffrage parade. She and other women **picketed** in front of the White House starting in 1917. They also handcuffed themselves to the White House fence and refused to move. Many were arrested. After being arrested during one protest, Paul went on a hunger strike. Because she refused to eat, she was sentenced to seven months in a mental hospital.

Women marched on foot and rode on horseback in a 1913 suffrage parade in Washington, D.C.

Ida B. Wells-Barnett

Ida B. Wells-Barnett was an African-American woman who lived in Chicago, Illinois. She fought for the right of African-American women to vote. African

Americans were not allowed to join the NAWSA because members of the NAWSA thought that if they included African-American women, it would hurt their chances of gaining the vote. So, in 1913, Wells-Barnett formed the Alpha Suffrage Club. She spent much of her time traveling through Illinois holding meetings to educate black women about why they should fight for suffrage.

Ida B. Wells-Barnett fought for women's suffrage and for basic rights for African Americans.

In March 1913, Wells-Barnett and other club members attended a suffrage parade in Washington, D.C. Because they were African American, they were told to march at the end of the parade instead of with the white **suffragists.** After a few minutes of arguing for her rightful place in line, Wells-Barnett walked away from the white suffragists. They assumed she had gone to march at the end of the parade. But as they marched down Pennsylvania Avenue, Wells-Barnett suddenly came out of the crowd of spectators and joined the few white women who had previously agreed that she should march with them. A photograph of Wells-Barnett marching with the others appeared in the next edition of *The Chicago Daily Tribune*.

PROGRESSIVISM

The suffrage movement helped women become aware of social issues, including food and drug safety, child labor, and worker safety. The movement concerned with these problems was called Progressivism and began during the 1890s. By 1900, it had spread across the nation. The men and women involved in Progressivism wanted suffrage for women, because social issues were important to women, and the movement needed their votes. Some businesses, however, were against Progressivism, because they did not want to spend the money necessary to clean up their factories and mines and to hire adult laborers instead of children.

Women in World War I

World War I began in Europe in 1914, but the United States did not enter the war until April 16, 1917. Five days later, on April 21, the government announced that it was forming the Committee on Women's Defense Work. One of the members of the committee was Carrie Chapman Catt, who was president of the NAWSA at the time.

The purpose of the committee was to find a way for American women to coordinate their activities and organize their efforts. During the war, women worked as both employees and volunteers. As men went off to war, women took their jobs. More jobs were created by the war, particularly jobs in factories where war supplies were made.

During WWI, women began to run family businesses, trained as nurses, planted gardens to feed their families and neighbors, worked in factories, and performed many other duties to keep the country going. These women are building a wing tip for an airplane.

About 13,000 women joined the Navy, Marine Corps, and Coast Guard—the Army did not yet have a procedure for women to join. By the end of the war, more than 30,000 women had served in the armed services—many as nurses. Their bravery and willingness to serve their country were, in part, what convinced President Woodrow Wilson that women should be given the right to vote.

A winning plan

Carrie Chapman Catt saw the war as an opportunity to achieve her association's goal of getting the vote for women through a federal **amendment.** She asked the NAWSA to support the country's efforts in preparing for war, and the members agreed. It was well known to everyone who knew her that Catt was against war, so many felt that her support of World War I was a kind of betrayal of her beliefs. She had a strategy, though, which she called "The Winning Plan." Catt knew that if the members spoke out against the war, they would be seen as unpatriotic, and the **suffrage** movement would be hurt.

Catt was praised as a patriot for her support of the war effort. She also made it known that because women had worked so hard, they deserved something in return—the vote. In 1918, President Wilson agreed and encouraged his fellow Democrats to pass the Nineteenth Amendment giving women the vote.

A PARTNERSHIP

After World War I ended in 1918, President Wilson said the following about women who served in the war and the fact that they could not vote:

Are we alone to ask and take the utmost that our women can give, service and sacrifice of every kind, and still say we do not see what title that gives them to stand by our sides in the guidance of the affairs of their nations and ours? We have made partners of the women in this war; shall we admit them only to a partnership of suffering and sacrifice and toil and not to a partnership of privilege and right?

The first **picket** line was organized in 1917. The women were urging President Wilson to support women's suffrage.

Passing the Amendment

On June 4, 1919, Congress finally approved the Nineteenth **Amendment.** To be added to the Constitution, the amendment had to be **ratified** by 36 states. Many states ratified the amendment almost immediately. By June 1920, 35 states had approved the Nineteenth Amendment. Only one more state was needed for it to become law.

There was one problem, however. The **legislatures** of all of the states had ended for the summer, and no legislature planned to meet before the November 1920 presidential election.

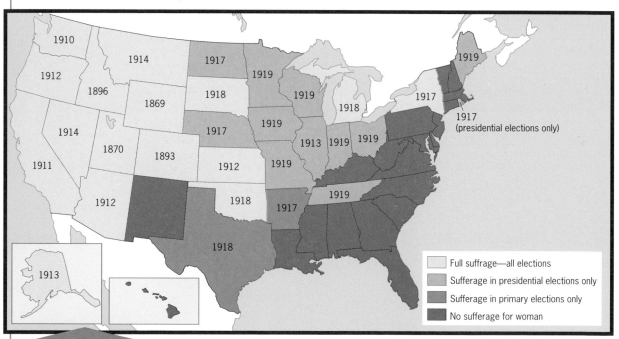

These are the dates when each state gave women the right to vote, before suffrage for women became national law in 1920.

1910
1914
1917
1919
1919
1912
1919
1918
1919
1896
1918
1917
1869
1917
1919
1914
1917
1913 1919 1919
1870
1893
1911
1912
1919
1912
1919
1918
1919
1912
1918
1917

1913

- Full suffrage—all elections
- Suffrage in presidential elections only
- Suffrage in primary elections only
- No suffrage for woman

1917 (presidential elections only)

Legislators in Connecticut and Vermont made it known that if their governors would call special legislative sessions, they would approve the amendment. But the governors of both states were against women's **suffrage** and refused to do so. President Wilson used his influence to get the governors of North Carolina and Tennessee to call special sessions. North Carolina rejected the amendment, so ratification in Tennessee became the only hope of getting the amendment through in 1920.

The Tennessee vote

When they found out that the Tennessee session would be sometime in August, many pro-suffrage and antisuffrage groups traveled to Nashville, the state's capital. The antisuffrage movement included big businesses such as the liquor industry and the cotton industry. Some people were also against suffrage because it would give voting rights to African-American women. African-American men could already vote, and some people did not want to give African Americans more power.

Many in Tennessee were pro-suffrage. Starting in 1919, women could vote in city elections and in presidential elections in the state. But people who were against suffrage put pressure on the legislators. Carrie Chapman Catt and members of the NAWSA were there and asked many of the legislators how they planned to vote. They discovered that the vote would be very close, and that possibly the **antisuffragists** would win by a single vote.

A mother's advice to her son

The night before the vote, a Tennessee legislator named Harry Burn received a letter from his mother, Febb King Ensminger Burn. Although most of the people in Burn's district were against women's suffrage, Mrs. Burn urged her son to vote for it if his vote would decide whether the amendment was ratified. He did, and the amendment passed. If Burn had voted "no," there would have been a tie, and the amendment would not have passed. The results of the vote were sent to Washington, D.C. It was announced on August 26, 1920, that the amendment had been added to the United States Constitution.

Women suffragists display a flag honoring the ratification of the Nineteenth Amendment.

The Equal Rights Amendment

In 1913 Alice Paul formed the National Woman's Party to support equal rights, including **suffrage,** for women. The 72-year battle to get the Nineteenth **Amendment** passed and **ratified** had taught her something. In 1923, just three years after the Nineteenth Amendment was ratified, Paul felt the need to write an amendment reinforcing the idea that the Constitution applied to all citizens of the United States, both male and female. She called it the "Lucretia Mott Amendment." The passage of the amendment, she and her supporters concluded, would ensure that a battle like the one they had just won would not have to be fought again.

The new amendment, which Paul submitted to Congress, stated: "Men and women shall have equal rights throughout the United States and every place subject to its jurisdiction." In the early 1940s, Paul rewrote the amendment, which is now called the Equal Rights Amendment (ERA). The new amendment states: "Equality of rights under the law shall not be denied or abridged [limited] by the United States or any state on account of sex."

Alice Paul, author of the Equal Rights Amendment, is shown here at a 1923 feminist rally.

The ERA was presented to Congress every year from 1923 to 1972, when it finally passed. The next step was to send the amendment to states to be ratified. But many people were against passing it.

Some people who had worked to get laws protecting women in the workplace thought the amendment would change those laws. Others were worried that passage of the ERA meant that women would be sent to war. Others feared that its passage would force universities that had been all-male for hundreds of years to start accepting female students.

The Equal Rights Amendment has been reintroduced to Congress every year since 1982, but has still not been ratified. Over the years, many women have held demonstrations in its favor.

To be added to the Constitution, the amendment needed to be ratified by 38 states. Twenty-two states ratified the ERA in 1972. But by the time the seven-year limit for ratification had passed, only 35 states had ratified the ERA, so it was not added to the Constitution. Those working for its passage asked Congress for an extension. While Congress did vote to extend the ratification limit to June 30, 1982, the ERA was still not ratified.

Women Make a Difference

The passage of the Nineteenth **Amendment** was a true turning point in U.S. history. For the first time, women in every state could vote in every election. Women began to feel that their opinions were finally respected. This gave them confidence to speak out in other areas of life as well.

Speaking out

Women began to speak out against social and political issues, and because women could now vote, politicians were forced to listen to them. As more women began to work outside the home, they began to push for safer working conditions and shorter workdays. They also wanted politicians to make sure the water they and their families drank and the food they ate was safe. Education was another important issue for women. They wanted to know that their children went to clean, safe schools. Many women had not graduated from high school and wanted a better education for their children.

Former First Lady Eleanor Roosevelt is shown here using a voting machine in 1925. Ms. Roosevelt not only voted in elections, but was also highly involved in social reform.

Women also wanted better health care for their children. While wealthy and middle-class families could afford doctors and hospitals, poor families often could not. Women began to ask the government to form agencies to help the poor. Eleanor Roosevelt, the wife of President Franklin D. Roosevelt, traveled to poor areas and crowded factories. She saw how the poor were forced to live, and she helped her husband develop a program called the "New Deal," which was to help those who could not find jobs.

As women became more involved in political and social issues, they began to be taken seriously in the workplace. For one thing, more and more women were going to college. In the 1920s, though, most women—even those with college degrees—had low-paying jobs, working as office typists or operating sewing machines in factories. Employers did not want to hire women, regardless of whether they were married or single, because they felt that they were taking jobs away from men who had to support their families.

Even today, few women make as much money as men do. On average, a woman earns about 75 cents for every dollar a man makes.

THE LEAGUE OF WOMEN VOTERS

In 1920, six months before the Nineteenth Amendment was **ratified,** Carrie Chapman Catt founded the League of Women Voters. She created the new organization to help women as they used their new voting power. The organization is still active today. It does not support any particular candidate or political party. Instead, it educates women about the political process in the United States and encourages them to be active in politics. Members of the League also work together on issues that are important to them. These issues have included **reforms** in child labor laws, minimum wage laws, environmental problems, homelessness, and education.

Soon after the League of Women Voters was established, women from Minnesota delivered a mile-long signature **petition** to its headquarters to send to Washington, D.C.

Women in Government

Since the Nineteenth **Amendment** was passed, women have been holding increasingly important roles in government. Jeannette Rankin was elected to represent the state of Montana in Congress even before women could vote. She was a representative from 1917 to 1919, and again from 1940 to 1943. Rankin fought for women's **suffrage** and was known for her antiwar views.

In 1932, Hattie Ophelia Wyatt became the first woman elected to the U.S. Senate. She represented the state of Arkansas. Her husband was a senator, and when he died she was appointed by the governor of Arkansas to replace him. In the election of 1938, she ran for office and was reelected for another six-year term.

Jeannette Rankin is shown here at a formal ceremony held in 1918.

In 1974, when Ella Tambussi Grasso was chosen as governor of Connecticut, she became the first woman to be elected governor without following her husband into office. The first African-American woman to serve in Congress was Shirley Chisholm, who represented New York from 1969 to 1983. In 2000, Hilary Rodham Clinton became the first former First Lady elected to the Senate when she won a New York election.

Women have also been appointed to positions in presidential **cabinets.** The first woman to serve in the president's cabinet was Frances Perkins, who was secretary of labor under Franklin D. Roosevelt from 1933 to 1945. Madeleine Albright was secretary of state under President Bill Clinton from 1997 to 2001. Clinton also appointed Janet Reno, making her the first woman to be attorney general. President George W. Bush appointed Condoleezza Rice, an African-American woman, to the high-level position of National Security Advisor.

A WOMAN FOR PRESIDENT?

Women make up more than half the population of the United States, but their numbers in government do not reflect that. A woman has never been president of the U.S. In 1984, New York Congresswoman Geraldine Ferraro ran for vice president with presidential candidate Walter Mondale, but they lost to Ronald Reagan and George H. Bush. Former U.S. Secretary of State Madeleine Albright once said, *"It is only a matter of time before we have a woman President of the United States."* Many Americans agree.

Women have led other countries. From 1979 to 1990, Margaret Thatcher held the highest governmental position in Great Britain, prime minister. India's first female prime minister was Indira Gandhi, who held the post from 1966 to 1977 and again from 1980 to 1984. Corazon Aquino—the first female president of the Philippines—held office from 1986 to 1992.

Madeleine Albright is the woman who has held the highest office in the U.S. government.

Important Dates

1834		Oberlin College becomes first college in the United States to allow women to attend classes
1840		Elizabeth Cady Stanton and Lucretia Mott decide to form a woman's rights society
1848	July 19–20	First Woman's Rights Convention
1868	July 9	Fourteenth **Amendment ratified**
1869		Elizabeth Cady Stanton and Susan B. Anthony form National Woman **Suffrage** Association; Lucy Stone forms American Woman Suffrage Association; Fifteenth Amendment ratified
1878		Suffrage amendment is first introduced to Congress
1880		Women's Christian **Temperance** Union supports suffrage
1890		American Woman Suffrage Association and National Woman Suffrage Association unify to become National American Woman's Suffrage Association
1913		Alice Paul forms National Woman's Party
1916		Jeannette Rankin becomes first woman elected to U.S. Congress
1917	April 16	United States declares war on Germany, enters World War I
1919	June 4	Congress approves Nineteenth Amendment
1920	August 26	Nineteenth Amendment ratified
1923		Alice Paul writes Equal Rights Amendment
1932		Hattie Ophelia Wyatt first woman elected to U.S. Senate
1968		Shirley Chisholm becomes the first African-American woman elected to Congress
1974		Ella Tambussi Grasso elected governor of Connecticut

Glossary

abolition   doing away with slavery; people who believed in abolition were called *abolitionists*

amendment   change in a law as a result of a formal voting procedure

antisuffragist   person against giving women the vote

cabinet   group of advisers

Civil War   in the U.S., the Civil War took place from 1861 to 1865 between the northern, or Union, states and southern, or Confederate, states

custody   charge or control

legislator   person elected to represent a state or a region of that state

legislature   group of people appointed or elected to make laws

petition   formal, written request, often signed by many people

picket   organized demonstration; people who picket often carry signs stating the reason for their protest

proclamation   formal statement

prohibition   forbidding the manufacture and sale of alcoholic beverages

Quaker   member of the Society of Friends, a Christian church that is against war and for equality

ratify   vote to approve something

reform   official change from one policy to another, or any change in a policy

resolution   statement of a formal stand on something, voted on by the members of the organization or association

saloon   business where alcoholic beverages are sold and consumed; bar or lounge

suffrage   right to vote

suffragist   someone who fights for the right to vote for oneself or for others

temperance   when someone does not drink alcoholic drinks

universal suffrage   voting rights for all adult persons, regardless or race, religion, or gender

Further Reading

Harvey, Miles. *Women's Voting Rights: Story of the Nineteenth Amendment.* Danbury, Conn.: Children's Press, 1996.

Isaacs, Sally Senzell. *America in the Time of Susan B. Anthony.* Chicago: Heinemann Library, 2000.

Parker, Barbara Keevil. *Susan B. Anthony: Daring to Vote.* Brookfield, Conn.: Millbrook Press, 1998.

Index